Study Skills

Discover How To Easily Learn Anything In The Most Effective & Time Efficient Ways Possible

By Ace McCloud

Copyright © 2014

Disclaimer

The information provided in this book is designed to provide helpful information on the subjects discussed. This book is not meant to be used, nor should it be used, to diagnose or treat any medical condition. For diagnosis or treatment of any medical problem, consult your own physician. The publisher and author are not responsible for any specific health or allergy needs that may require medical supervision and are not liable for any damages or negative consequences from any treatment, action, application or preparation, to any person reading or following the information in this book. Any references included are provided for informational purposes only. Readers should be aware that any websites or links listed in this book may change.

Table of Contents

Introduction 6
Chapter 1: Getting Excited to Learn 8
Chapter 2: Methods of Success 13
Chapter 3: Study Tools and Resources 24
Chapter 4: Your Ultimate Learning Action Plan 27
Conclusion 29
My Other Books and Audio Books 30

Be sure to check out my website for all my Books and Audio books.

www.AcesEbooks.com

Introduction

I want to thank you and congratulate you for buying the book, "Study Skills: Discover How To Easily Learn Anything in the Most Effective and Time Efficient Ways Possible."

Being able to learn information as efficiently and quickly as possible is a critical skill that can pay huge dividends throughout your entire life. Nothing is quite as frustrating as spending hours on end trying to learn a new subject, only to forget half of it a few weeks later. In the modern age, with the world's knowledge at our fingertips, those who truly succeed and thrive will be those who can easily assimilate all of the abundant information available and then utilize that knowledge strategically and intelligently for peak performance results!

Think back to your time in grade school—can you recall those who seemed to be "naturals" at getting good grades and those who struggled to keep up? In which group did you fit in? If you've never really felt like a high-achieving, naturally "smart" person, you can change that with the knowledge in this book. The truth is that anyone can master the right skills and techniques that are best for learning and anybody can use those skills to increase their learning potential!

Discovering how to improve your study skills is not just important for getting good grades in school—the better you can program your brain to absorb and analyze information as well as connect multiple thoughts and ideas together will help you in life for as long as you live! However, if you are still in school, it is crucial to tap into your inner genius now—your grades often have a big influence on where you will end up after graduation. High school students with low grades will have less of a chance of getting into the college of their choice and college students may not be able to snag an internship or could end up putting themselves through tremendous pain and aggravation just to barely get by and graduate.

Most importantly, your grades tend to reflect what kind of person you are—if others see that you can achieve high grades, they will know that you are most likely a hardworking, detail-oriented person who stays committed to their obligations and goals. Getting good grades can also make school more fun. You'll feel great about yourself knowing that you can set your mind to a goal and achieve it.

Don't mistake this for a magic guide on how to study for 10 minutes and get amazing grades. While it is true that studying can take a lot of time and effort, there are ways to do it intelligently and in the *least amount of time possible*. This requires learning good time management skills to make the most out of the time that you *do* spend studying along with utilizing top-of-the-line brain-mind techniques that you will learn about later in this book. Time is precious and you can never get it back—that is why it is so important to learn study skills that are effective and efficient. Whether you are a student or a college graduate, these skills you are about to learn will give you the competitive advantage needed today! It's now time to truly open up the world of possibilities for yourself!

Chapter 1: Getting Excited to Learn

Before you can jump into the amazing world of learning and studying, there are a few steps that you'll need to take to get yourself set up. Studying is an art and if you know how to get started, you can truly unlock your inner genius and absorb all of the information you want like a sponge. This chapter will take you through some in-depth strategies that you can use to set yourself up for success. Let's start with the basics...

Treat School like your Career. If your only obligation is to go to school, treat it like your career. Like a job, you go to school [almost] every day. Although there is wide debate on whether college is a waste of time/money, I have come up with my own theory. Your degree isn't going to be a magic piece of paper that will automatically get you a job when you produce it to your prospective employers. Rather, your degree is a symbol of the underlying traits that you can bring to the table. Obtaining a degree shows that you have what it takes to work hard, stay committed to a task, and follow through with your obligations. That's really what prospective employers want. Treat school as a career and focus on the practical skills you can bring to the table once you graduate. That being said, make sure you act like you're an employee of your curriculum. We'll get to more on this later on.

Take Risks, Take Charge, and Take Pride. Treat your education as your responsibility. Doing this early on can do wonders for your attitude and be very helpful in your future career. Put yourself out there and take risks—don't think you would do very well in a statistics class? Try it anyway. Trying can only help you improve. My one friend is really great at English and liberal arts but terrible at applied sciences like math and science. When she was in college, she had to take a statistics class as a requirement for her major. She was really nervous and not looking forward to it at all, but she went ahead and took it to get it out of the way. To her surprise, she ended up getting a "B," totally shocking to her as she would usually get F's and D's when it came to math. She was able to do this by using some of the strategies that you will discover later in this book. School is a great place to discover what your strengths and weaknesses are so that you can try and avoid things that you're weak at in the future and strive towards those areas in which you excel.

Be Passionate. Although this can be tricky, try to be passionate about your classes. For first-year students or those who haven't picked a major yet, it might be a little difficult to get into those general requirement classes. However, try to find something interesting in each one of your classes that will help you stay motivated until the end of the semester. If you've already a picked a major, it is much easier to be passionate about what you're learning. Always evaluate your passion for your major every year to make sure that you haven't lost your love for it. For more advanced information on maintaining your passion, be sure to check out my books on <u>Motivation</u> and <u>Inspiration</u>.

Set Academic Goals. Without goals, your educational journey can go awry. My same friend, who was nervous about taking a math class, didn't bother to set any academic goals during her first two years of college. Instead, she got distracted by the many kinds of classes her school offered. Eager to learn about multiple new topics, she didn't put much time into planning her major and she almost ended up having to spend an extra year in school just to get enough graduation credits toward her major. Many colleges have different requirements for different majors so it is imperative to plan as early as you can. For example, if you want to be a psychology major, you will have to look at the psychology department catalog for your school and figure out how many psychology credits you will need to take each semester to graduate on time. Sometimes, you might have to apply to a major, and that will take up extra time. Check with your school for specific requirements.

It is also a good idea to start off each goal with the phrase: "I will easily..." You should have a specific timeframe for the completion of the goal and a motivating factor as to "why" you want to get this goal accomplished. It's a good idea to review all your goals every day. For goal making like a professional, I highly recommend the goal setting program: Goals On Track.

Practice Good Time Management Skills. Studying will take up a lot of your time so it is important to get into the habit of practicing good time management skills. A great idea is to keep an agenda where you can organize your homework, curriculum, and anything else that will help you excel. Make up a basic schedule based off your daily routine and make some special time for studying. This might mean you have to cut back on spending time doing other things, such as socializing, but with the right amount of work, you can come up with a perfect, awesome schedule. For more information on how to perfect and manage your time management skills, check out my bestseller: Ultimate Productivity.

Establish Strong Relationships With Your Teachers. The more you feel like you can approach your teacher, the more likely you will be to succeed in school. In college, most teachers hold office hours where you can drop by and talk to them. Some students go to office hours to ask questions about the course material while other students go just to talk. No matter what you go to office hours for, building a strong relationship with your teacher can help you become motivated to study harder. Your teacher will also see how serious/interested you are in the course material and may be more willing to help you excel. It's always a good idea to have your teacher on your side.

Getting Ready Physically

It is especially important for students to take care of their bodies. When you're away at college, it can be tempting to stay up all night, party, go without eating right, or a combination of those things. However, the better you take care of yourself and your body, the better you will be able to focus on studying. Eating right and sleeping right can make all the difference in your alertness.

The recommended amount of sleep for an average student is 8 hours per night. It is a good idea to get into a routine sleeping pattern because it can boost your overall health and productivity. For example, if your earliest class is at 8:00 am and you have to wake up at 6:00 am on that day, you should wake up at 6:00 am every day. The same goes for picking a time to go to bed. When your body gets used to a sleep pattern, it will be able to function better. Sleeping in until the afternoon one day and getting up at the crack of dawn the next day can really mess up your body!

It is also important to eat healthy and stay hydrated. If you've got a meal plan at your school, it can be tempting to over eat on unhealthy things. Most college dining halls serve up a variety of food including pizza, French fries, fried chicken, salads, stir fry, vegetarian options, fruits and vegetables, and of course, desserts. The bigger your school, the more likely they are to have a wider range of foods, because they will have to meet the needs of certain diets (for example, a school that has a large population of Jewish students might have a kosher section). The key to eating healthy in school is to just be aware of what and how much you're putting in your body.

Breakfast is the most important meal of the day. Whatever you do, don't skip it! Make sure you wake up early enough to get some food into your body. Try to make sure that you have some good sources of protein in your breakfast. Most dining halls offer a variety of eggs, pancakes, French toast, bacon, hot and cold cereals, and fruit. Some good ideas for breakfast would be to have a hard-boiled egg, some fruit, and a glass of skim milk or a bowl of hot oatmeal with berries on top and a glass of skim milk. Avoid things like bacon, home fries, donuts, or anything else that isn't going to power your body.

When it comes to lunch and dinner, just be smart. Healthy, brain-boosting foods usually include poultry, fish, leafy greens, fruits and vegetables, and whole grains. Depending on what your school serves, make sure you load up on skinless chicken, lean meats, fish (salmon is the best), dark greens such as spinach, pastas (whole grain if possible), and vegetables. If you're a salad person, make yourself a nice, big salad with lots of healthy toppings such as light dressing, grilled chicken, a handful of shredded cheese, and/or fresh vegetables.

Avoid the soda fountain and go for a healthier choice like water or milk. Also, try to avoid sugary juices or sports drinks. Some schools offer different kinds of milk, like almond milk and soy milk for those who have special diets. If you commit yourself to eating right, your body and brain can become a powerhouse and you'll have a much easier time focusing, concentrating, and absorbing information.

Finally, don't forget to exercise while you're at school. It can be as simple as walking to your class instead of taking the shuttle bus or simply going to the gym. Most schools have a gym that is free for students to use. Schools that are huge sometimes have 3 or 4 gyms! Exercising can help keep your mental stress down while boosting your energy at the same time. Some students find ways to exercise in their dorm rooms. Some of the newer video game systems have games that promote exercise so if you have a system and some exercising games, don't forget to bring them along for those cold, rainy days where you just don't want to go outside.

If you are truly serious about being healthy and keeping a high energy level throughout the day, then be sure to check out my best-selling books: <u>Ultimate Health Secrets</u> and <u>Ultimate Energy</u>.

Setting Up Your Environment

Aromatherapy. Aromatherapy can not only make your room smell nice but it can also reduce stress and clear your brain so that you can study more efficiently. Studies show that aromatherapy can help strengthen your memory and recollection as well as improve your concentration. Additionally, it can help improve your ability to sleep. The best way to engage in aromatherapy is to invest in a small <u>oil diffuser</u> and experiment with different oils. Some of the best oils that you can use to achieve mental clarity are <u>peppermint</u>, <u>rosemary</u>, <u>juniper berry</u>, and <u>sage</u>.

Brainwave Music. Brainwave music is a combination of waves that helps your brain absorb information for storage in your long-term memory banks. The frequencies in brainwave music tracks help balance your brain into a state in which it can learn better. For the best results, you should listen to these tracks using headphones. Here are some great ones on YouTube that you can try out:

<u>Study Smarter Not Harder</u>
<u>Study Aid Binaural Beats</u>
<u>Binaural Beats: Focus, Concentrate, Study Music</u>
<u>Study Aid For Super Learning and Memory</u>

Finding a Quiet Place. Finding a quiet place to study is crucial for being able to focus. When you're surrounded by loud noise or other distractions, it can be difficult to retain other information. The library is a great place to study but you can also just turn off your electronics and study in your room. Some dorms also have designated quiet study areas. Other people might like to sit outside and study.

Practice Good Posture. When you're learning or studying, it can be tempting to slouch or kick your feet up. However, you might want to break those bad habits. Not only can practicing good posture directly affect your brain, it can also reduce your chances of stiff muscles. Good posture uses less energy, which means you can put more towards learning. Your posture correlates with your hormones, so the taller you sit, the more confident and powerful you are likely to feel.

Organizing. If your work area is littered with clutter, you may actually end up becoming stressed out. Mental stress can put a damper on your ability to focus and concentrate. It can also make you waste time by searching for the materials you need. Make sure that your work area is free of clutter and everything is where it should be before you start studying. Also be sure to turn off your electronics and eliminate any other distractions.

Chapter 2: Methods of Success

Now that you know how to prepare yourself for learning, the next step is to go over some great tricks and tips that will help you succeed. In this chapter, you will discover some of the best techniques for quick and efficient learning.

Use an Agenda. Before you even go to class, buy an agenda or assignment book for the year and use it to plan out your schedule. You can plan ahead for big projects, final papers, and exams. You can also use it to figure out when you should study.

Bring in a Positive Attitude. Another thing you should bring to school with you is a positive attitude. If you begin with an attitude of, "I hate school and I'm not going to get good grades," then good luck because that's exactly the result you will likely McCloudget. However, if you come in with a more positive attitude, one that says something like, "I'm really going to try my hardest this semester and do what I can to continuously improve," odds are you will have a much more favorable outcome.

Dealing With Teachers the Smart Way. Dealing with teachers as a student can be just as tricky as dealing with bosses as an employee. You will probably have some teachers that either you don't like or who don't like you. Don't just drop the class because you think it won't be an "easy A." Learning to work with your teachers regardless of what kind of relationship you have is important for priming yourself to be successful. Another strategy is to figure out your teachers. As a student, you'll have a variety of teachers and they're likely all to be different. Some base your grade off participation and others will just focus on your test scores. Get to know the expectations of your teachers and adjust your strategies accordingly. You are bound to be much more successful if you know what your teacher wants and he put in the extra effort to give it to them.

Seating Matters! When you sit in the far back of your classroom, it can be easy to goof-off or not pay attention. This is especially true in large college lectures where there may up to 300 students in your class. For optimal learning, sit within the first three rows of seating. In large lecture halls, research has shown that if you sit somewhere in a "T" shape, you will get the most out of your class. So for a classroom that has three seating sections (the middle and two wings), try to sit within the first three rows and envision yourself sitting in a "T" shape.

But wait—what if your teacher assigns you a seat? What if your last name starts with an S and you get stuck all the way in the back anyway? Simply ask to have your seat changed. Let your teacher know that it is hard for you to focus all the way in the back.

Once you've found a seat that works for you, be sure to practice good posture. It can be tempting to slump in your seat and stretch your legs out, but that can make you feel tired and less likely to pay attention. Sit with your back straight and upright. Sometimes it helps to keep a bottle of water with you to stay hydrated. When you sit up straight, you will be able to see what's going on at the front of the classroom, which can help you pay attention better.

One last note—avoid sitting near distractions. Try not to sit near students who use laptops, move around a lot, fidget with food and drinks, etc. If you have a crush on somebody, don't sit too close to them either or you might end up studying and thinking about them instead of the course material.

Find a Study Buddy. Your classmates can be a valuable source of "study power." When you study with one or more people, your brain is more likely to remember the material. Many students like to get together in study groups, especially when exam time is nearing. Study groups can be a fun and memorable way to learn and memorize your notes. Always try to make at least one friend in every class. This way, you can help each other and pick each other's brains all semester. If you join a study group, just make sure it doesn't turn into a social group. If you find that this is happening, it may be time to look for some new study friends.

Limit Your Extracurricular Activities. Participating in a few extracurricular activities can be a great thing, but if you go overboard with it, you risk not having enough time to devote to your education. Limit yourself to only participating in activities that are extra important to you. If you can, try and align them with your education. For example, if you're a science major, you might consider joining the environmental club.

Do Your Homework. It can be especially tempting to not do your homework, especially in college, because half of the time it doesn't necessarily get graded. However, it is important that you do it anyway! The purpose of homework is to reinforce what you've learned in class. Whether it is just reading a few chapters out of your textbook or answering some questions, actively participating in your homework can help prime your brain to learn the material better. Sometimes your teachers end up grading the homework anyway and that can have an effect on your grade, so always do it.

Don't Procrastinate. Procrastination is a huge time waster, so avoid it at all costs! Homework and studying can sound like a damper but it is very important to getting good grades. Do whatever it takes—turn off electronics, make up a declaration, or pick a role model that you can use for motivation. Sometimes you will need your laptop for studying, so make sure you close out all of your "distracting" websites such as Facebook, Twitter, YouTube, etc.

Read the Class Syllabus. Teachers generally hand out a syllabus on the first day of classes. This is a piece of paper or two that gives you a schedule of the class and an idea of what you're going to learn. The syllabus tells you most everything you need to know, including your teacher's office hours, the supplies you will need, what the course is about, and how the course will flow. Always keep your syllabus handy so that you can be on top of the game. My friend used to use hers to plan out when all of the important assignments in her classes were due and she would get them done ahead of time to make room for more studying. One time, she was even able to use one to read an entire book during the summer before her class even began.

Set Goals. Set both long-term and short-term goals for yourself. In some cases, you can set short-term goals to work toward a long-term goal. For example, if your long-term goal is to become an English major, your short-term goals could be to complete the credit requirements over the course of 4 years. You could even break it into more specific short-term goals. For example, if your specific long-term goal was to become an English major with a 4.0 GPA, your short-term goals could be to make your English classes first priority so that you can get all A's. If you are looking for professional goal setting program then I highly recommend: Goals On Track.

Actually Go To Class. Some students brag about the fact that they don't go to class and that they can still get a good grade. However, by not going to class you are cheating yourself out of an educational opportunity. Going to glass can actually be fun and you'll learn so much more than by just reading the book. Most of the time, teachers will put questions on their tests that you can only get right if you go to class anyway.

If you can, try to have perfect attendance. The less material you miss, the better you will do on tests and exams. However, sometimes unforeseeable events will arise that will make it hard for you to go to class. If you get sick or if you have to miss class for some reason, be sure to email or meet with your teacher so that you can get the most out of the lecture that you will be missing.

Do Extra Credit. Most of the time, you will probably have an extra credit opportunity or two. Go for it. Extra credit not only boosts your grade but it also helps you remember the material better and it shows your teacher that you are willing to go above and beyond with your education. You never know—you might need those couple of extra points to bring a B+ up to an A.

Keep Your Attention Span in Check. It can be easy and tempting to zone out in the middle of class. When you find this happening to you, do something to get back into focus. Take a drink of water, stretch in your chair, or take a quick walk outside (just don't make it too long or you might miss important notes). Doing these things can help you get back in focus.

Use a Timer. If you are the type of person who might spend too much time studying one subject and not another, invest in a small timer—there might even be one on your phone. Set out specific blocks of time for studying based on the demands of your schedule. Whenever you go to study, set your timer so that you do not take up more time then you intended.

Schedule Ahead. Schedule your bigger assignments a few days ahead of time so that you can be absolutely sure you finish and perfect them. So, if you have a big paper that is due on the first of the month, pretend like it is due on the 27th of the previous month and schedule it in your agenda that way. By doing this, you can give yourself ample time to get it done and you will have extra time at the end to go back and make it amazing.

Take Breaks in Between Studying. When you're studying by yourself, your eyes can easily glaze over after a short time. You start by really focusing on the reading but then next thing you know, your eyes are just scanning it and you're not absorbing any information at all. When this happens, give yourself a break—you don't have to study for 4 hours straight. Take a walk, grab some food, do something for fun, and then go back to what you were doing.

Turn Off Electronics. Turn off your cell phone, laptop, tablet, or anything else that may be distracting. Some students argue that they use their laptop to take better notes but I think it's just another distraction. If you pay attention and write your notes down, your chances of remembering them are much better. Invest in a nice watch so you don't have to use your cell phone to check the time. Some students also like to bring a voice recorder with them, but I also think that creates more work. Taking notes by hand means you can underline, circle, and star things, and you'll only have to take the notes once. Recording a lecture means you will have to transcribe it or listen to it again

Take Courses That Will Challenge You. If you try to load up on "easy A" classes, you risk the chance of growing bored. When you grow bored with a class, it can be very hard to pay attention, study, and even go to the class. To avoid this, take classes that pose a challenge to you. Most schools have an advisory department where you can meet with a mentor who can help you figure out the best courses to take.

Be an Active Listener. Listening and hearing are two different things. Your ears function in a way that you hear everything around you—but it can easily go over your head. Be sure that you are focused and engaged in your teacher's lecture. Taking notes helps.

Take Good Notes. Taking good notes is essential for doing well in most classes and learning situations. Most college professors make their exams based off their lecture, so note-taking is a must. One great idea for developing great note-taking skills is to print the lecture slides beforehand (if your professor provides them) and take notes on those. More techniques include creating your own shorthand for quick writing, creating an outline of your notes, and noting any key themes that your professor talks about during the class. Don't write in complete sentences and integrate drawings into your notes. It's also a good idea to come up with your own personalized abbreviations for key words that come up often.

Remember, you can't write down everything, so be an active listener and write down what is key. If your professor repeats something a few times, put a star next to it because it will most likely show up on the test. After class, go over your notes to refresh yourself and even take more notes on your notes. This is a good technique for preparing ahead of time for your tests. Always make sure that your notes make the most sense to you. Another good strategy is to borrow a friend or classmate's notes to see if they caught something you may have missed. If you prefer, you may rewrite your notes if they are not organized well. This can also help you remember them better.

Read the Textbook. Sometimes your professor might make you buy the textbook for his or her class and not even have you open it. However, your textbook is often a goldmine of information. Don't fall into the trap of "speed reading" or "highlighter reading." It is important to learn how to become an effective reader. As you're reading, it is important to take notes, just as if you were in class. As you read, analyze the chapter and ask yourself how it fits into your class and your professor's lecture. It is easier to identify key terms in your textbook because they are often in bold. If you really want to process the information, write a reaction to the reading. Answer questions such as, "what are the most important parts of this?" or "what is my emotional reaction?"

Actively Participate. When you go to class, make sure you participate. If you're uncomfortable answering or asking a question in front of your class, wait for small group discussions or go to your teacher before/after class. If you go to class to just sit there, odds are you'll zone out easier and you will not understand the material as well.

Read Selectively Instead of Speedily. Speed reading can be useful but it is mostly ineffective because you don't have the chance to absorb what you're reading. Skimming is a better option. To be a successful skimmer, make sure you read the introduction, conclusion, and summary paragraphs of your text. For every other paragraph, read the first and last line. Take advantage of studying any graphs or charts that might be within the chapter.

Discuss Course Material. By discussing the course material with another classmate, you can actively process the information. This method can allow you to teach one another as if you were in class without feeling the pressure of being graded.

Visualize. Visualization is a powerful technique. You can use it to help yourself ace your tests. Close your eyes and use all your senses to visualize where you will be in life if you do well in school. Imagine what you'll see, hear, feel, taste, and even smell. The more detailed you can visualize, the more powerful it can be. Visualization is a great way to help yourself stay motivated to study. It's also a good idea to visualize yourself in the third person, as if you were three or four feet away from yourself, actually doing the studying and then seeing the great results later on with a good grade or incredible test score.

Don't Try to Outsmart Your Teacher. Your teachers are smart. They know all of the oldest tricks in the book, like making the periods in your paper size 14 font to make it longer. By doing that, you're not only disrespecting your teacher but you're also disrespecting yourself. Don't cheat yourself out of knowledge—there's always something to write about!

Don't Waste Time Worrying. If you worry about school, you could be using up valuable time for learning. Worrying will never get you anywhere but studying and trying will. Learn how to avoid worrying as part of your time management techniques and make the most of your time. If you're going to spend time worrying, try using that time to practice relaxation methods to make it more worthwhile. Yoga and meditation are some great ways to relax and you can do them right in your dorm room. Exercise is also a great way to beat stress. Laughter therapy is also an incredible way to relieve stress and bring more joy into your life.

Be Prepared to Fight Off Panic Attacks. If you are a worrier and you are not skilled at managing your mental stress, it is possible to have a panic attack, especially in the days leading up to a big test or project. Remind yourself that although your grades are important, they are not a matter of an emergency. If you *don't* do as well as you had hoped, remind yourself that nobody is 100% perfect and use the experience to study harder for next time. When you begin to panic and worry, it can spread to other students, so it is best to control your panic attacks and paranoid thoughts before they spread. Instead, try to spread positive thoughts with the hopes that they will come back to you. While many people will put a lot of pressure on your academic success, no single class or test is actually really all that important in the long run. As long as you don't give up, there will always be a chance for redemption.

Don't Burn Bridges With Teachers. You might really dislike your teacher, making it tempting to end your class on a bad note or burn a bridge. However, many college professors teach multiple classes and you never know if you'll get stuck with them again. If you've given them a bad impression, they will be less likely to help you succeed. I have encountered a few teachers in my academic career that were truly not there for the right reasons. They made their students' lives miserable and they were miserable people themselves. In these cases just do your best to survive the situation and let that teacher's superiors know of your unpleasant experience. Who knows, your feedback may be able to get this teacher replaced with someone who is actually a great teacher and save hundreds or even thousands of other students from the torture of dealing with this one bad seed teacher. I even had teachers from a prestigious university who could not even speak English clearly in high level classes! So annoying! In situations like this, be sure to let your opinion be known to those who are supposed to be making the students the number one priority!

Know What Research Materials to Use. When you're researching a topic or looking to learn more about something, the source that you refer to can make a huge difference. The best sources of correct, accurate information often come in the form of scholarly articles, lab reports, or other textbooks. Information you find on the web may not always be accurate. Your library should also have some reliable sources.

Become a Great Researcher. As a researcher, it is up to you to find the best information possible on a subject and report about it. Anybody can easily find general information using the internet but you can make yourself stand out by knowing the secrets to great research skills (and you'll learn more, too!). The main piece of advice is to always be a skeptic. Always question your sources and pick them down as much as possible.

It's always easier to research a specific topic. Let's pretend that you're taking a sociology class and you've chosen to write a paper on drugs. Now, there is so much information and subtopics on "drugs" that it would be impossible to read through it all and pick out the best things to talk about. In that case, it is always best to narrow the topic. Let's say that you decide to write a paper on the social effects of marijuana on society. Now you have a niche to work with.

Next, you'll need to pick a thesis statement, which is the overall argument of your paper that you will be trying to prove. A good thesis statement for this said paper could be something like, "Does marijuana have a negative effect on society?" (That's an average thesis example only being used to help you gain an idea. Yours can be much more specific).

When it comes to researching facts on that statement, you'll then know to focus on books and scholarly articles based on marijuana and society. A good idea would be to look for research studies, current statistics and trends, and maybe even some newspaper articles that you can use as real life examples.

When you've found some sources to use, analyze them to make sure they are of quality content. For example, pay attention to any statistics that you use. If you want to use a statistic that says, "75% of people who use marijuana have reported a decrease in their ability to stay motivated," research that statistic. Find out how many people were interviewed. If the study that found that statistic only interviewed 5 people and 3 out of 5 people reported feeling unmotivated, the statistic suddenly becomes too narrow and possibly invalid. Look out for statistics that are based on large groups of people, because they will come off as more valid. Also, don't leave out other facts. For example, while 3 out of 5 people may have felt less motivated, four out of five people could of reported feeling a decrease in overall pain levels and an increase in their creativity.

Any references that you find in scholarly journals are usually great resources because they're written by experts. Good places to start are scholarly article databases such as EBSCOhost and Google Scholar. Your school's library may also have a database. Books are usually good sources as well. Always be sure to research the author to make sure that their credentials are legitimate.

Follow these simple tips whenever you're researching a subject for the best material so that you can get a great grade and an awesome dose of high-quality knowledge.

Study With Flashcards. Flashcards can be effective study tools, especially when you have to memorize many different key terms. Flashcards help you because making them lets your brain process the information and you can adjust your deck based off your studying needs. Sometimes you can even buy pre-printed flash cards (for example, you may be able to buy these for a basic Spanish class). You can carry your flashcards around with you and quiz yourself whenever you have free time. You can quiz yourself both ways—by identifying the key term by its definition or the definition by its term. These are very effective study tool and highly recommended.

Create "Master" Lists. When you're studying at home and organizing your notes, make master lists of key terms, themes, and anything else that you find is relevant to the class. Not only will this help your brain process information but it can be a useful tool for studying right up to the minutes before your exam.

Look For Old Exams. Sometimes, you can find an old exam from a previous class that your professor taught. Usually these exams are posted online for the use of a study aid. Another good way to find these is to ask upperclassmen who may have taken the same class before. When you do this, take extra caution not to be looking for the current exam—that could lead to big trouble and possibly get yourself kicked out of school.

Memorize Things with Literary Tricks. Some people find it helpful to memorize things by creating rhymes or using alliteration. You can also come up with a mnemonic device. For example, a common way that people remember the different stages of biology is to use the acronym "Kings play cards on fat green stools." The first letter of each word represents an actual word: in this case, it stands for Kingdom, Phylum, Class, Order, Family, Genus, Species. This is another highly effective strategy and highly recommended! Be sure to use your creativity and come up with cool phrases that you can easily remember and that help make learning fun.

Memorize Things with Mental Associations. If you can remember something by mentally associating it with an image, then you have found an effective way to study. There is no right way to do this, as everyone may associate words with different images, but it is definitely a powerful method that students have been using for years. Once again, be creative and come up with interesting images that you can easily remember and that will allow you to have fun during the learning process. For example, if you are trying to memorize the common math equation: pi equals MC squared, you could visualize a giant cherry pie on a seesaw perfectly balanced with MC squared as a giant sign in the hands of a human stick figure sitting on the other side of the seesaw.

Make a Special Schedule Before Exams. Before your mid-term and final exams, prepare a special study schedule that you can use to really get the most out of everything you've learned. You might find that you want to spend a few more hours of time studying each class you're taking in order to prepare for your tests. After your tests, you can go back to a normal schedule.

Read Your Notes Before Tests. As you wait for your professor to arrive and hand out your exam, use the free time to read over your notes again. Don't use the time to worry about whether you will pass the exam, otherwise you would just be wasting useful time. Always try and keep a positive attitude and always try to be thinking of the most productive thing that you could be doing. If negative thoughts creeping in, just overwhelm them with positive incantations that you can repeat silently in your head, such as: "I'm super smart and I'm excellent at taking tests."

Read the Directions. For both homework and tests, always read the directions of the assignment. There is nothing worse than spending time on an assignment just to find out that you've completely missed the point. Reading the directions is important because it will save you from having to start over and you will be learning the right information, which usually comes in extremely handy around test time.

Don't Jump Into Tests. When you get your exam, it can be tempting to just dive into it right away. However, if you jump too quickly and speed through it, you may end up doing a bad job. When you receive your exam, take a few minutes to read through the questions. Usually your professor will ask anybody if they have questions related to the test. Take note of how the test is structured and what the point value of each question is. Note how long you have to take the exam and try to allocate enough time for each section. Don't rush, whatever you do—most schools give you enough time successfully complete a test. When you're finished, look it over, twice in some sections, before handing it in. It is easily possible to make a mistake. If you can catch it, you will not lose points for something silly.

If You Don't Know an Answer, Spend Some Time on it and Guess. If you don't know the answer to a test question, don't skip it over. If it's an essay, take a shot at it anyway. It is better to receive some credit than none for not even trying. It is easier to guess multiple choice questions because you can often easily eliminate some of the answers. True or false questions can be a little trickier, but just try to be logical. For example, if a statement says, "x never happens," just think of a reasonable example where it does happen and you'll be able to guess that the answer is false. When it comes to writing an essay, it is helpful to write down some notes on what you know about the question. If you have a choice of essays, pick the one that you're most knowledgeable on.

Reward Yourself. Rewarding yourself can be a great way to stay motivated when it comes to studying. If you try to barrel through it without stopping to rest or have some fun, your attempts might not be effective. Many students find the idea of having some "free time" to themselves as the ultimate reward, but it can be anything you want. Take breaks in between large chunks of studying and work your way through it. For example, if you can get through reading 3 chapters of something, take a break and have a milkshake and then go back to studying.

Take Pride in Your Work and Never Give Up. Sometimes, school can be tough, really tough. Sometimes you just get stuck with a difficult teacher. Sometimes you just want to throw your hands up and say, "forget this!" It's so tempting and easy but it's the wrong way out. The key is to learn from your mistakes, never give up, and own your work. Here is a story to help give you a better perspective:

My friend, who I have mentioned several times in this book, was faced with a huge challenge during her junior year of college. As a requirement for her major, she had to take a business writing class. She picked out a class with a teacher that had rave reviews on the website RateMyProfessor.com. Well, the teacher turned out to be a real nightmare! The big project of the class was to create a mock business plan for an invention or idea that could be implemented on campus.

My friend had a difficult time coming up with an idea for her business plan but she figured out something awesome. When the students shared their ideas in class the next day, her teacher basically told her that the idea was too broad and to narrow it, so my friend did. The mid-term project was to create the first draft of the business plan. My friend, knowing that the teacher wasn't really a fan of her in the first place, worked as hard as she ever did on the project. When she got the paper back, there was a big comment on it from the teacher saying, "Did I even approve of this topic?" My friend met with the teacher after class to say, "Yes, you did, and I even narrowed the topic when you asked." The teacher then told her that she didn't spend enough time on the paper and it would take a lot more work than she had put into it. My friend wanted to burst out crying, and another girl who went up to talk to the teacher actually did.

Wanting to just drop the class but knowing she had to take it for her major, my friend went all out to work on the final project, which included the written business plan and an oral presentation. She worked on it for weeks. The day came for her final presentation and my friend went up in front of the class and owned it. While everyone else used notes for their oral presentation, my friend did it 100% from memory and engaged the audience by moving her hands and talking in a casual tone. When the presentation was over, all of the students clapped and told her how interesting and great her project was. Even the teacher said, "Wow! Great job! You really blew it away!" My friend felt so great about herself!

She ended up with a "C" for the class anyway and that kind of upset her, knowing how much she committed herself to conquering that class and the teacher, but the moral of the story is that she never gave up. She could have easily dropped the class and taken it again at a later date, but she wouldn't let the teacher scare her off. She might have gotten a "C" in that class but the experience she got was priceless. She learned how to deal with and overcome a difficult situation despite the fact that she had an easy way out. She took pride in her work despite it having been slammed and insulted along the way. She didn't let the teacher put a damper on her energetic speaking skills. Sometimes, it's not about the grade itself, but the valuable experience that you get from your class—experiences that you can use to conquer the real world once you get there.

Chapter 3: Study Tools and Resources

This chapter will give you some insight on some great tools and resources that you can use to boost your studying power and prepare yourself for getting the best results.

Supplements

Supplements are a great tool for giving your brain and body an extra health boost. There are many natural supplements that you can take to stay healthy and keep your brain a studying powerhouse. This section will give you some great ideas on the different kinds of supplements that you can take to help you study and get stellar grades. As always, you should talk with your doctor before deciding to take any type of natural supplement.

Some supplements, such as Focus Formula, are specifically designed to enhance your brain functioning and memory. These supplements are packed with natural vitamins and herbs that can boost your memory, concentration, and information processing for when you need to study. Ginko Biloba is also another great supplement especially good for boosting your memory. Supplements like these are also known to balance out your hormones so that your mood stays stable. Finally, they promote extra oxygen flow to your brain so that your attention span lasts longer. Focus formula and other natural supplements are safe for all ages as long as they are taken in the proper dosages.

If you are having trouble sleeping, you might also want to consider a natural supplement. Melatonin is something that your body produces naturally but you can also take it in pill form. Melatonin helps regulate your sleep cycle so that you can establish a regular sleeping routine. Valerian Root is also a good alternative supplement to cure insomnia and other sleeping problems. If your living area is extra noisy, you also might want to invest in a box of earplugs.

Finally, it is important to take care of your body in general. If you let yourself get run down, your chances of coming down with a cold or the flu worsen, especially if you're around a lot of people. Schools and colleges are loaded with germs and it is easy to catch something. It is much harder to study and concentrate when you're sick. In addition to eating right and exercising, you can opt to take a multivitamin to ensure that your body is getting all the nutrients and minerals it needs. Since our genders and bodies function differently, there are multivitamins made for both men and women.

Organization Tools

When you're in school, there is nothing better to help you study than some great organization tools. When you're organized, it is so much easier to focus and concentrate on the subject material. If you're not sure what you need to get done or where to begin, you risk wasting precious time that you could be putting toward your schoolwork. This section will go over some great organizational tools that you can use to boost your studying skills.

I can't stress enough how important it is to have an agenda. You can use it to map out your homework, short-term assignments, long-term assignments, and goals. Consider getting an agenda that is designed to help you stay organized and reach your goals, such as this Results Planner. These types of agendas run a little more expensive than your basic ones but they are so much more effective. Whatever agenda you choose, make sure that it is for the correct school year and that it has sections for you to write out your tasks, plan your goals, and write in notes.

Speaking of organization, it is also a good idea to keep your workspace clear of clutter. The more clutter in your work area, the more stressed out you are likely to be and the more stressed you are, the less you will get done. Keep your pens and pencils in one area, your notes in another, and so on. One specific tool that I would recommend is this Multifunction Alarm Clock. It's an all-in-one tool that has everything you need while you're away at school. You can use the alarm clock to ensure that you wake up on time every day and you can keep your pens, pencils, and highlighters together inside of it. It's even got a built-in calendar to help you keep track of the days. I think this tool could be really, really helpful for a college student. Plus, it's small, so you can easily fit it right on your desk.

Finally, in the world of organization, it is a good idea to keep your course material separate. So if you're taking a math class, a history class, and a music class, you can keep your notes for each class in separate notebooks/folders. That way, when you go to study, you can go right to the designated notebook or folder and quickly gain access to all of your notes. To do this, you can get a 5-subject notebook that has built-in dividers and pocket folders. This way, you don't have to sift through individual notebooks; you can carry all of your notes around with you at the same time.

Self-Improvement Books

Reading self-improvement books is not only useful for studying but it can be useful for living an overall great life. There is so much information to absorb. The better you feel about yourself, the more likely you are to believe in yourself and bring out the best of your abilities. When it comes to studying, there's nothing like feeling confident, inspired, creative, motivated, productive, or healthy! You might even consider brushing up on your self-discipline skills!

Subliminal Reprogramming

What if there was a way to easily "reprogram" your mind to instantly unlock your inner genius and other creative skills without any effort at all? You actually can with a great program called Subliminal Power. This software is a windows program that runs in the background of your PC while you use it. During the time that it runs, it flashes subliminal affirmations to you through your screen. While you can't see it with your eyes, your subconscious will pick it up. The software is very vast and allows you to work on several self-improvement areas of your life, including your study skills. You can even design your own subliminal programs while custom tailoring them with pictures.

YouTube Videos

Lastly, here are some great YouTube videos to help you sharpen your skills. Visual aids and videos are a great alternative to reading and can serve as a great break for your eyes. Here are some of the best videos that I believe can help you strengthen your study skills.

How to Study For a Test by watchwellcast
How to Take Great Notes by watchwellcast
5 Tips to Get Better Grades by Improve Your Study Skills
Study Skills: How Your Memory Works by MrStudyTV
How to Stay Super Motivated When Studying by MrStudyTV

Chapter 4: Your Ultimate Learning Action Plan

Now that you've discovered all of the great tips, strategies, and tools on how to develop your study skills and get the most out of your education, it is time to figure out how to bring it all together to get a stellar report card. This chapter will help you put it all into perspective with the help of an ultimate learning action plan. You can follow the one in this book directly or use it as a model to create your own. Start to develop your action plan as early as possible—preferably starting from the first day of classes.

Step 1: Before even going to your classes, make sure you are prepared with everything. Pick out folders and notebooks to dedicate to each class. Fill your backpack with pens, pencils, paper, sticky notes, calculators, highlighters, and any other supplies that you might need for the semester. If you are able to view your class syllabus online before you go to class for the first time, look it over and make sure that you have everything your teacher asks for.

Step 2: At the end of the first week of classes, make sure you're organized. Keep all your syllabuses and notes in their designated folders/notebooks. Go through your syllabuses and plan out all of your long-term projects in your agenda, aiming for a due date that is earlier than the actual due date. Start to develop a schedule based on your classes, including a designated time for sleeping, eating, and studying.

Step 3: Talk to your teacher and try to find out what their exams are like so you can prepare yourself ahead of time. Ask them or look online for sample tests so you can get a feel for what you're up against. Make sure you know the date, time, and location of your exams even if they're a few months away. Add them to your agenda if you haven't already.

Step 4: Consistently follow your study schedule using the methods outlined in Chapter 2. In between that, make sure that you are eating right, sleeping right, and exercising a few times a week. You might also want to use this time to look for some study groups to join. Make sure that you are paying extra attention to your notes.

Step 5: About a week before your exam, start to get into hardcore study mode. Refer to all of your notes (you'll thank yourself for taking such great notes) and use them to start making your master lists. This will reinforce the information processing part of your brain so that you can recall the information more quickly. Allocate at least four hours per class to do this.

Step 6: With at least 5 days until your exams, and no more than two days before, start to make flashcards so that you can test yourself. Use your master lists to identify any general themes of your class, because you might find yourself faced with an essay regarding this theme. Prepare any last-minute questions that you may have for your professor and communicate with them. Most professors have extended office hours in the days leading up to exams. Double check and confirm the exam location in case a room change has been made.

Step 7: During the last 24 hours before your exam, review your master lists again and try to identify any themes that might show up as essays. Pay extra attention to any concepts that you are still having trouble with. Pack your backpack with extra pens, pencils, your calculator, a bottle of water, and anything else you might need. Go to bed extra early and make certain that you will wake up for your alarm. Set two if you are a heavy sleeper.

Step 8: Before you take your exam, make sure that you eat a great breakfast that is packed with plenty of protein. Avoid sugary foods or anything that might make your brain crash. Go to your classroom a few minutes early and talk with some of your classmates about the course material to warm yourself up. Relax and do your best!

Step 9: After your exams are all done, reward yourself and do something fun for all your hard work! Many students look forward to going back home for Christmas break after mid-term exams and if it's your final exams that you have just taken, do a fun, summer-related activity. Think about what your reward will be ahead of time so that you can stay motivated to study hard.

Step 10: Watch out for your grades to be posted and give yourself a pat on the back when you see your hard work reflected in your report card. Repeat for the next semester and be sure to use the skills you have learned throughout the rest of your life!

Conclusion

I hope this book was able to help you to discover some great ideas on how to study smarter and make the most out of your valuable time. Sharpening up your study skills may be a little more challenging than it seems, but it certainly pays off. It is a long process that requires intelligent preparation, including eating right, exercising, getting enough sleep, using the best study skills and keeping your life/environment organized. As you now know, there are many great strategies that you can experiment with to create the ultimate learning experience for yourself.

The next step is to set up an action plan like the one you just read about in Chapter 4. As you are preparing for your next project or semester in school, write out your own action plan with personalized details of the most intelligent ways to proceed. Don't forget to put yourself in a positive, powerful state of mind right before doing this. Look in the mirror and tell yourself that you will strengthen your study skills, get the most out of your education, and get good grades. Imagine what you will be able to do with all of your new-found knowledge and skills. The future will truly be yours to command if you can put everything together and learn anything that you wish to study like a pro! Be sure to make the most important things that work well for you and give you positive results a habit and you are sure to have great results all throughout your life!

Finally, if you discovered at least one thing that has helped you or that you think would be beneficial to someone else, be sure to take a few seconds to easily post a quick positive review. As an author, your positive feedback is desperately needed. Your highly valuable five star reviews are like a river of golden joy flowing through a sunny forest of mighty trees and beautiful flowers! *To do your good deed in making the world a better place by helping others with your valuable insight, just leave a nice review.*

My Other Books and Audio Books
www.AcesEbooks.com

Peak Performance Books

Health Books

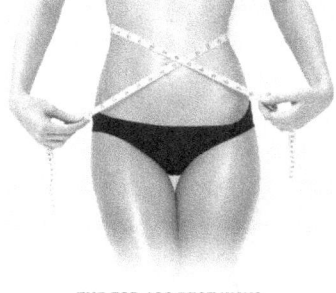

Be sure to check out my audio books as well!

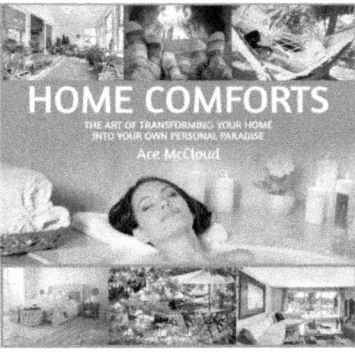

Check out my website at: **www.AcesEbooks.com** for a complete list of all of my books and high quality audio books. I enjoy bringing you the best knowledge in the world and wish you the best in using this information to make your journey through life better and more enjoyable! **Best of luck to you!**